Great Day

Written by Sarah Prince
Illustrated by Bettina Guthridge

sundance™
A Haights Cross Communications ® Company

"It's a beautiful day," said Dad.
"What if we go to the zoo?"

"Great," said Sam.

3

We went on the bus to the zoo,
but the bus broke down.

We had to wait
and catch the next bus.

4

When we got to the zoo,
we stood in a line for a ticket.

Jo dropped her money,
and it rolled down the drain.
She started to cry.

7

We went to see the monkeys.
Uncle Vin dropped his camera,
and the monkeys jumped around.

Uncle Vin screamed.
The monkeys screamed.
The zookeeper screamed.

We ate our lunch on the grass.
Sam stood on a sandwich
and got honey on his shoe.

Jo spilled her orange juice
on Mom's dress.

We went to see the lions.
On the way, Sam got lost.

Dad went to look for him.
Dad got lost, too.

13

"Let's go for a walk," Mom said.

But on the way it began to rain.

"What if we go home?" said Dad.